Sunshine

Pupil's Book 3

Ausgabe Bayern

Erarbeitet von
Stefanie Aschkar (Konstanz)
Tanja Beattie (Ebersberg)
Nadine Kerler (Ulm)
Caroline Schröder (München)

Auf der Grundlage der Ausgabe von
Birgit Hollbrügge
und Ulrike Kraaz

Cornelsen

Contents

listen to your partner or teacher

listen to the CD, Track 1

read

talk

play

draw or write

extra

blue words you need to know

1 Read the words. Find the pictures.
computer, cowboy, mountain bike, skateboard.

2 Do you know more words? Make a poster.
Think. Pair. Share.

! Note

🇩🇪	🇬🇧
Cornflakes	cornflakes
Jeans	jeans

1 Listen. Look at the numbers. Point to the pictures.

Say the rhyme with a partner.
Do the actions.

Meeting friends

Note

In Großbritannien sind alle Briefkästen rot. Fallen dir weitere Besonderheiten auf?

1 Talk about the picture.

2 Listen to your teacher.
Point to the numbers.
Say the colours.

black · blue · brown · green · grey · orange · pink · red · white · yellow

3 Listen. Where do they live?

What colours do you like?
Make a list.

Door number 3 is yellow.

Number … is Harry's house.

1 Listen. Point to the numbers.

2 Say the numbers.

3 Explain the rules.

4 Play 'hopscotch'.

5 Read the dialogue with a partner.

1 Talk about Harry's family. Say: *This is …*

2 Listen. Point to the pictures.

Write about your family: *I've got …*

baby
brother
family
father
grandfather
grandmother
mother
sister

Let's talk

3 Read the dialogue. Talk to a partner.

Write your own dialogue.

1 Look at the map. Where do they speak English?

Talk about the colours and the flags.

Listen to your partner. Point to the country.

Pets in the garden

Note

People drink a lot of tea in Britain.

18 **1** Listen. Who is on the phone?

Let's talk

2 Read the dialogue. Talk to a partner.

☆ Write your own dialogue.

1 Listen. What pets do the children have?

2 Make a class survey. *How many children have got a pet?*

Write sentences: *Emily has got a ... / It's a ... / I've got a ...*

Think. Pair. Share.

cat · dog · fish · guinea pig · hamster · mouse · pets · rat

1 Read the story.

2 Act out the story.

Write a party invitation.

Dear Hamster,
can you come to my party?

Yes, thank you. ☒
No, I'm sorry. ☐

From Rabbit

1 Read the words and sentences.

2 Explain the rules.

3 Play the game.

1 Listen. Point to the pictures.

1

sheep dog

2

rescue dog

3

police dog

4
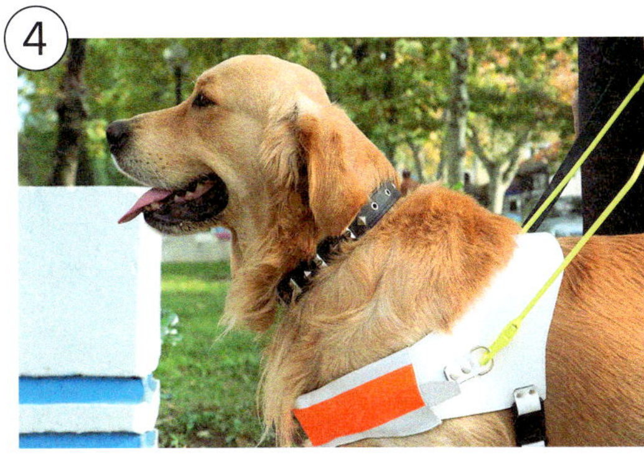
guide dog

2 Read the speech bubbles with a partner.

3 Do the dog actions with your partner. Guess the actions. Take turns.

4 Guess the actions in class.

→ DVD 2

3 At school

1 Talk about the classroom. Where's Mr Mole?

2 Listen to the song. Point to the school things in the picture.

☆ Where are the school things? Write sentences:
The chair is next to the table. Think. Pair. Share.

Where's Mr Mole?	*Is he in the school bag?*
Where can he be?	*Is he on the book?*
Where's Mr Mole?	*Is he under the table?*
Let me see.	*Let's have a look.*
	No! Not there!

book · chair · classroom · pen · pencil · rubber · school bag · scissors · table · teacher

Note

In vielen Klassen in Großbritannien gibt es einen zweiten Lehrer oder eine zweite Lehrerin. Diese Person nennt man *classroom assistant*.

1 Read the texts.

2 Explain the rules.

3 Play the game in groups of 4.

(1) Take 5 cards from your word box.

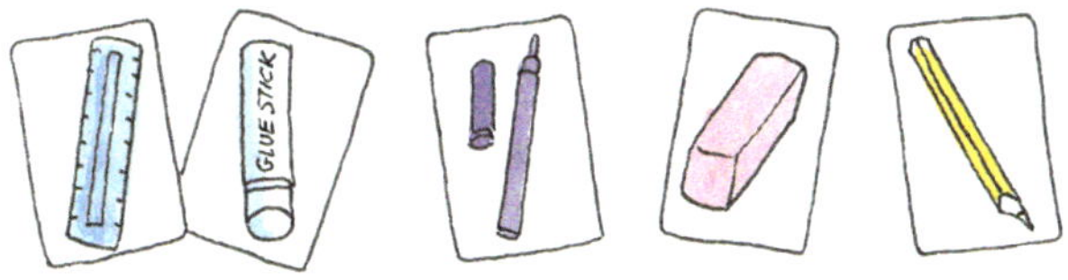

(2) Put your cards on the table.

(3) Shuffle all the cards.

(4) Give 5 cards to each player.

(5) Ask questions.

The player with the most cards wins.

Story: Jack's bad day

1 Listen to the story.

2 Read the story.

3 What happens in the end? Think. Pair. Share.

→ DVD 3

Note

In England schaust du zuerst nach rechts, wenn du eine Straße überquerst. Weißt du warum?

1 Talk about the pictures.

2 Listen. Point to the pictures. (32)

3 Read the texts.

A **lollipop man** helps children cross the road.

Some children walk to school with the **walking bus**.

This is a **school building**.

School starts with **assembly**.

4 Make a school badge. You need:

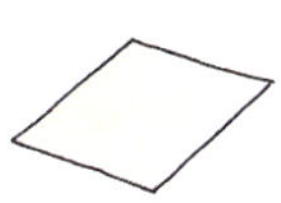 cardboard	 felt tips or coloured pencils	 scissors	 a safety pin	 sticky tape

(1) Draw a circle on the cardboard. Write your school's name. Colour the badge.

(2) Cut out the badge.

(3) Tape a safety pin to the back of your badge.

→ DVD 4

What I can do and say

A word web

family

brother
mother
father
sister

This is my …
I've got a …
I haven't got a …

grandfather …

How many … have you got?

Make your own word web

Think. Pair. Share.

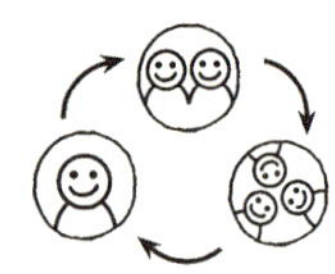

school

pets

friends and family

My name is … · This is my … · It's a … · It likes … · What colour is … / do you like? · Its name is … · I'm … · What about you? · Where are you from? · I'm from … · I'm in class … · My teacher is … · Can I have …, please? · Here you are. · Thanks. · You're welcome. · My favourite …

What can you do or say in English? Think!

I can …

- … say the words.
- … write the words.
- … ask and answer questions.

What do you want to be better at?

What I can do and say

You can find more words

- in your Pupil's Book.

Word list — Englisch – Deutsch

A
apple Apfel
B
banana Banane
bedroom Schlafzimmer
behind hinter
big groß
bike Fahrrad
birthday Geburtstag
birthday cake Geburtstagskuchen
birthday card Geburtstagskarte
birthday present Geburtstagsgeschenk
black schwarz
blackboard Tafel
blue blau

Easter bunny Osterhase
Easter egg Osterei
eat essen
eight acht
eighty achtzig
F
family Familie
father Vater
Father Christmas Weihnachtsmann
favourite Lieblings-
felt tip Filzstift
fifty fünfzig
fish Fisch
five fünf
food Essen

- in your Activity Book.

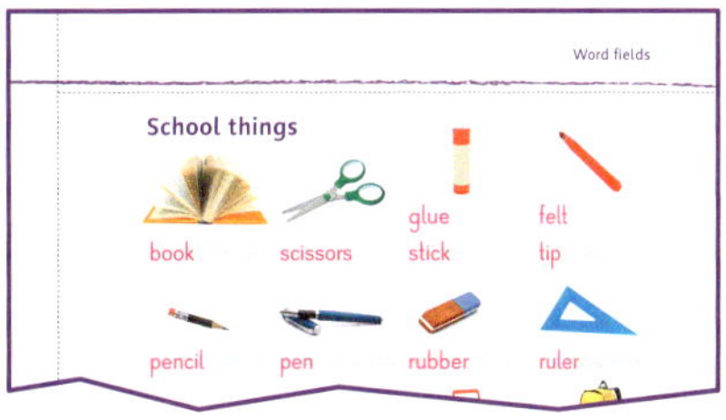

- in a dictionary.

- on the Internet.

Play 'pick a pair' with your mini picture cards.

Game for 2 players. You need: 2 sets of mini picture cards

(1) Put the cards on the table.

(2) Pick 2 cards. Turn them over. Name the cards.

(3) 2 cards the same? Keep the pair and play again.

(4) Not the same? Put them back again.

The player with the most cards wins.

4 The second-hand shop

1 Talk about the picture. Say: *I can see …*

Listen to your partner.
Find the clothes in the picture.

I can see …

dress · jeans · pullover · shirt · shoes · skirt · trousers

Note

jeans – Jeans

Can you find more words that are the same in German and English?

1 Listen to your teacher. Who is it?

2 Play 'I spy'. Explain the rules.

☆ What is Samir wearing? Write: *He is wearing …*

Note

she (girl)

he (boy)

She is wearing a red dress. Who is it?

It's …

1

Sarah

2

Harry

3

Kate

4

Samir

5

Emily

6

John

Let's talk

1 Read the dialogue. Talk to a partner.

Write your own dialogue.

2 Talk to your partner. Ask: *Do you like ...?*

Write the words. Look at page 20 and your word list (page 41–44).

1 Read the story.

2 Act out the story.

Story: The smartest giant in town

40 **1** Listen to the story. Point to the pictures.

2 Talk about the pictures. How does the story end?

1

2

3

4

5

6

3 Read the rhyme. Find the matching pictures.

What about picture 6?

Find the rhyming words. Write a list.

My tie is a scarf for a cold giraffe,
My shirt's on a boat as a sail for a goat,
My shoe is a house for a little white mouse,
One of my socks is a bed for a fox,
My belt helped a dog who was crossing a bog,
But look me up and down –
I'm the smartest giant in town.

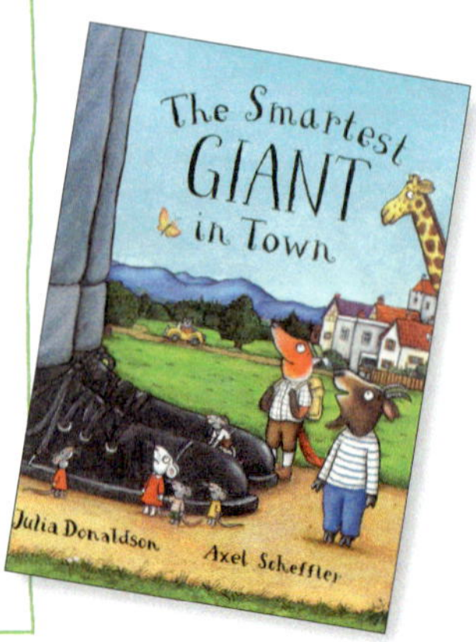

1 Talk about school uniforms. What is the boy wearing? What is the girl wearing? Say: *The girl is wearing ...*

a cardigan · a pullover · a shirt · shoes · a skirt · socks · a tie · trousers

Note

In Großbritannien tragen die Kinder Uniformen in der Schule.
In welchen Ländern gibt es noch Schuluniformen? Schaue im Internet.

41 **2** Listen. Point to the pictures.

Listen to your partner. What school is it?

1

2

3

Queen's School | Swanage School | Blake School

→ DVD 4

5 Free-time activities

43 **1** Listen to the song. Point to the pictures.

2 Sing the song. Do the actions.

☆ Make up a new song.

Think. Pair. Share.

bike · football · in-line skates · skateboard · snowboard · tennis

like · play · ride

1

2

3

Football, music, books, TV
Bikes and comics, friends, PC
Tell me, tell me,
What about you?
Do you like the things I do?

Playing football
Is what I like
Watching TV
Riding my bike.

Listening to music
Tapping my feet
Meeting friends
In the street.

Reading books
And comics, too
Playing computer games.
What about you?

4

5

6

Let's talk

1 Read the dialogue. Talk to a partner.

☆ Write your own dialogue.

2 Listen to the rhyme. Point to the pictures.

3 Read the rhyme.

☆ Make up your own rhyme. *Is it in …?*

Words for your rhyme:

ball · garden shed · painting · playing · toilet · wall

Where's the cat? Where's the cat?
Is it in the living room – watching TV?
Is it in the kitchen – drinking my tea?

Where's the cat? Where's the cat?
Is it in the bedroom – eating my shoe?
Is it in the bathroom – playing with shampoo?

Where's the cat? Where's the cat?
There it is – sleeping in my favourite hat.

1 Where's Harry?

2 Listen to your partner. Find the things in the pictures.

Write sentences: *There's ...* Look at your word list (page 41–44).

1

2

1 Listen to the story.
Point to the pictures.

2 Read the story.

3 Listen to the story. What don't they say?

1 Look at the pictures.
Read the names of the games.

2 Talk about the games.

50 **3** Listen. Point to the pictures.

Playground games:

connect 4 · hide and seek · skipping · tag

Note

Was spielst du gerne auf dem Schulhof? Vergleiche.

4 Read the rules. Explain the rules.

5 Play 'rock, paper, scissors'.

① Say and do.

Rock, paper, scissors. Show!

② Who's the winner?

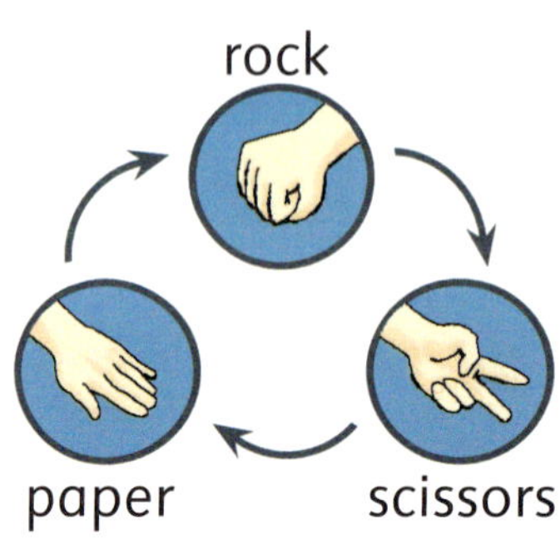

③ Two hands the same?

Play again!

In the park

1 Talk about the picture. Where is Mr Mole? Say: *I can see …*

☆ Listen to your teacher. Find the numbers.

☆ How many dogs / tables / scooters / … can you see? Write a list. Look at your word list (page 41–44).

☆ Talk about the picture. Say: *How much is …? – It's …*

56 **1** Listen. What does the boy say?

☆ Write a shopping list.

Let's talk

2 Read the dialogue. Talk to a partner.

☆ Write your own dialogue.

1 Listen to the story.

2 Read the speech bubbles.
Say what's right and what's wrong.

More to explore: Signs in the park

1 Look at the signs. Read the sentences. Match.

2 Talk about the signs.

Draw a new park sign. Write a sentence.

Think. Pair. Share.

1

2

3

4

5

6

Wheelchair access.

No ball games.

No drinking water.

No bikes.

No horse riding.

No dogs.

→ DVD 8

1 Talk about the picture.

2 Write a birthday card.

3 Sing the song. Do the actions.

59 **4** Listen to the song. Point to the pictures.

Someone's birthday is today, is today, is today.
Someone's birthday is today, and it's our …

Let's prepare a birthday cake,
Birthday cake, birthday cake.
Let's prepare a birthday cake,
Just for our …

Add a candle for each year,
For each year, for each year.
Add a candle for each year,
Just for our …

Make a special birthday card,
Birthday card, birthday card.
Make a special birthday card,
Just for our …

Note

Zum Geburtstag tragen englische Kinder gerne selbst gebastelte Hüte oder Kronen. Wie feierst du deinen Geburtstag?

Note

Kinder in Großbritannien hängen am 24.12. Strümpfe auf. Diese werden über Nacht gefüllt. Kennst Du weitere Besonderheiten?

1 Look at the picture. Talk about the Christmas things.

2 Look at the pictures. Find the Christmas things in the house.

1 Read the card.

2 Write a valentine card. Look at your Activity Book (page 46).

Who was Saint Valentine? Find out on the Internet.

3 Read the story with a partner.

Present it in class.

The world's smallest Valentine

It's Valentine's Day.
Olivia is visiting her granddad and grandma.

Olivia: This is for you, granddad.
Granddad: Oh, thank you. What is it?
Olivia: It's a valentine card.
Granddad: What's inside the card?
Olivia: A tomato seed.
Granddad: A tomato seed?
Olivia: Yes. The old name for tomato is 'love apple'.
Granddad: Thank you, Olivia. A love apple seed.
What a lovely Valentine!

Special days: Easter

66 **1** Listen to the rhyme.

2 Say the rhyme and do the actions.

> **Note** 
>
> In England essen die Leute zu Ostern *hot cross buns*. Was isst du gerne zu Ostern?

Here is a bunny
With ears so funny,

And here is his hole in the ground.

When a noise he hears,
He pricks up his ears,

And hops in his hole in the ground.

What I can do and say

A word web

clothes

dress
jeans
pullover
shirt
shoes

Do you like …?
Yes, I do.
No, I don't.
I like …
I don't like …
I' m …

cold …

How many … have you got?

Make your own word web. Think. Pair. Share.

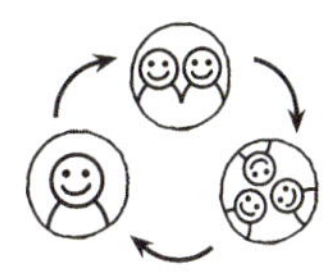

hobbies

special days

fruit and drinks

Can I help you? · Yes, please. · No, thank you. · I'd like… · Can I have … please? · Here you are. · You're welcome. · How much is …? · How many …? · Please come to my party. · Can you come to my party? · Yes, I can. · No, thank you. · I'm sorry. · That's ok. · What about you? · Merry Christmas! · Happy Birthday!

What can you do or say in English? Think!

I can …

… say the words.

… write the words.

… ask and answer questions.

What do you want to be better at?

What I can do and say

Can you write the word?

① Read the word.

② Look up.

③ Look at the word again.

④ Write down the word.

⑤ Check the word.

Play 'bingo'. with your mini picture cards.

Game for 3 or more (1 caller).
You need: 2 sets of mini picture cards for each player.

How to play:

① Put down 6 or 9 cards.

② Listen to the caller. Have you got the card? Turn it over. Listen again.

③ Have you got all cards? You are the winner.

A
apple Apfel

B
banana Banane
bedroom Schlafzimmer
behind hinter
big groß
bike Fahrrad
birthday Geburtstag
birthday cake Geburtstagskuchen
birthday card Geburtstagskarte
birthday present Geburtstagsgeschenk
black schwarz
blackboard Tafel
blue blau
book Buch
boring langweilig
boy Junge
bread Brot
brother Bruder
brown braun
Bye! Tschüss!

C
can/can't können/nicht können
candle Kerze
carrot Möhre
cat Katze
chair Stuhl
cherry Kirsche
chocolate Schokolade
Christmas Weihnachten
Christmas Day Weihnachtstag (25.12.)
Christmas Eve Heiligabend (24.12.)
Christmas tree Weihnachtsbaum
class Klasse
classroom Klassenzimmer
cold kalt
colour Farbe, ausmalen
come kommen

D
dog Hund
draw zeichnen
dress Kleid, ankleiden
drink Getränk, trinken

E
Easter Ostern
Easter basket Osterkorb
Easter bunny Osterhase
Easter egg Osterei
eat essen
eight acht
eighty achtzig

F
family Familie
father Vater
Father Christmas Weihnachtsmann
favourite Lieblings-
felt tip Filzstift
fifty fünfzig
fish Fisch
five fünf
food Essen
football Fußball
forty vierzig
four vier
friend Freund
fruit Obst

G
garden shed Gartenhaus
Germany Deutschland
girl Mädchen
gloves Handschuhe
glue stick Klebstift
good gut
grandfather Großvater
grandmother Großmutter
great toll
green grün
grey grau
guinea pig Meerschweinchen

H
hamster Hamster
happy glücklich
hat Mütze
here hier
hobby Hobby
house Haus

I
ice cream Eiscreme
in in
in front of vor
in-line skates Inlineskates

J
jacket Jacke
jeans Jeans
juice Saft

Word list

L
lemon Zitrone
lettuce Salat
like mögen
listening to music Musik hören
living room Wohnzimmer
lunch Mittagessen
lunch box Brotdose

M
meeting friends Freunde treffen
Merry Christmas! Frohe Weihnachten!
milk Milch
mother Mutter
mouse Maus

N
next to neben
nine neun
ninety neunzig
number Zahl

O
on auf
one eins
orange orange, Apfelsine

P
peach Pfirsich
peanuts Erdnüsse
pen Füller
pencil Bleistift
pencil case Federmappe
pencil sharpener Bleistiftspitzer
pet Haustier
pink rosa
play spielen
playing computer games Computerspiele spielen
playing football Fußball spielen
plum Pflaume
pound (£) Pfund (britisches Geld)
pullover Pullover

R
rabbit Kaninchen
rat Ratte
read lesen
red rot
reindeer Rentier
room Zimmer
rubber Radiergummi
ruler Lineal

S
scarf Schal
school Schule
school bag Schultasche
school bus Schulbus
scissors Schere
scooter Roller
seven sieben
seventy siebzig
shirt Hemd
shoes Schuhe
shop Laden
sister Schwester
six sechs
sixty sechzig
skateboard Skateboard
skirt Rock
small klein
snowboard Snowboard
socks Socken
stockings Strümpfe
strawberry Erdbeere
sweets Süßigkeiten

T
take nehmen
tea Tee
T-shirt T-Shirt
teacher Lehrer, Lehrerin
ten zehn
thirty dreißig
three drei
tomato Tomate
trousers Hose
twenty zwanzig
two zwei

U
under unter

V
very sehr

W
watching TV fernsehen
white weiß

Y
yellow gelb

Word list

Deutsch–Englisch

A
acht eight
achtzig eighty
ankleiden dress
Apfel apple
Apfelsine orange
auf on
ausmalen colour

B
Banane banana
blau blue
Bleistift pencil
Bleistiftspitzer pencil sharpener
braun brown
Brot bread
Brotdose lunch box
Bruder brother
Buch book

C
Computerspiele spielen playing computer games

D
Deutschland Germany
drei three
dreißig thirty

E
eins one
Eiscreme ice cream
Erdbeere strawberry
Erdnüsse peanuts
essen eat
Essen food

F
Fahrrad bike
Familie family
Farbe colour
Federmappe pencil case
fernsehen watching TV
Filzstift felt tip
Fisch fish
Freund friend
Freunde treffen meeting friends
Frohe Weihnachten! Merry Christmas!
Füller pen
fünf five
fünfzig fifty
Fußball football
Fußball spielen playing football

G
Gartenhaus garden shed
Geburtstag birthday
Geburtstagsgeschenk birthday present
Geburtstagskarte birthday card
Geburtstagskuchen birthday cake
gelb yellow
Getränk drink
glücklich happy
grau grey
groß big
Großvater grandfather
Großmutter grandmother
grün green
gut good

H
Hamster hamster
Handschuhe gloves
Haus house
Haustier pet
Heiligabend (24.12.) Christmas Eve
Hemd shirt
hier here
hinter behind
Hobby hobby
Hose trousers
Hund dog
hundert hundred

I
in in
Inlineskates in-line skates

J
Jacke jacket
Jeans jeans
Junge boy

K
kalt cold
Kaninchen rabbit
Katze cat
Kerze candle
Kirsche cherry
Klasse class
Klassenzimmer classroom
Klebestift glue stick
Kleid dress
klein small
kommen come
können can

Word list

Deutsch – Englisch

L

Laden shop
langweilig boring
Lehrer, Lehrerin teacher
lesen read
Lieblings- favourite
Lineal ruler

M

Mädchen girl
Maus mouse
Meerschweinchen guinea pig
Milch milk
Mittagessen lunch
mögen like
Möhre carrot
Musik hören listening to music
Mutter mother
Mütze hat

N

neben next to
nehmen take
neun nine
neunzig ninety

O

Obst fruit
Orange, orange orange
Osterei Easter egg
Osterhase Easter bunny
Osterkorb Easter basket
Ostern Easter

P

Pfirsich peach
Pflaume plum
Pfund (£) pound
Pullover pullover

R

Radiergummi rubber
Ratte rat
Rentier reindeer
Rock skirt
Roller scooter
rosa pink
rot red

S

Saft juice
Salat lettuce
Schere scissors
Schlafzimmer bedroom
Schokolade chocolate
Schuhe shoes
Schulbus school bus
Schule school
Schultasche school bag
schwarz black
Schwester sister
sechs six
sechzig sixty
sehr very
sieben seven
siebzig seventy
Skateboard skateboard
Snowboard snowboard
Socken socks
spielen play
Strümpfe stockings
Stuhl chair
Süßigkeiten sweets

T

T-Shirt T-shirt
Tafel blackboard
Tee tea
toll great
Tomate tomato
trinken drink
Tschüss! Bye!

U

unter under

V

Vater father
vier four
vierzig forty
vor in front of

W

Weihnachten Christmas
Weihnachtsbaum Christmas tree
Weihnachtsmann Father Christmas
Weihnachtstag (25.12.) Christmas Day
weiß white
Wohnzimmer living room

Z

Zahl number
zehn ten
zeichnen draw
Zimmer room
Zitrone lemon
zwanzig twenty
zwei two